D1490919

The Law of Attraction
Fifteen Historic Perspectives

The Law of Attraction
Fifteen Historic Perspectives

Genevieve Behrend, Elizabeth Towne, Prentice Mulford, William Walker Atkinson, Earnest Holmes, Wallace D. Wattles, James Allen, Ralph Waldo Trine, Orison Swett Marden, Thomas Troward, Joseph Murphy, Charles F. Haanel, Robert Collier, Theron Q. Dumont, and Napoleon Hill

Wilder Publications, LLC.
PO Box 3005
Radford VA 24143-3005

ISBN 10: 1-60459-089-0
ISBN 13: 978-1-60459-089-0

First Edition

10 9 8 7 6 5 4 3 2 1

Table of Contents

From Your Invisible Power
by Genevieve Behrend
ISBN: 1-934451-72-X

From the Edinburgh Lectures I had read something about the Law of Attraction, and from the Chapter of "Causes and Conditions" I had gleaned a vague idea of visualizing. So every night, before going to sleep, I made a mental picture of the desired $20,000. Twenty $1,000 bills were counted over each night in my bedroom, and then, with the idea of more emphatically impressing my mind with the fact that this twenty thousand dollars was for the purpose of going to England and studying with Troward, I wrote out my picture, saw myself buying my steamer ticket, walking up and down the ship's deck from New York to London, and, finally, saw myself accepted as Troward's pupil.

This process was repeated every morning and every evening, always impressing more and more fully upon my mind Troward's memorized statement: "My mind is a center of Divine operations." I endeavored to keep this statement in the back part of my consciousness all the time with no thought in mind as how the money might be obtained. Probably the reason why there was no thought of the avenues through which the money might reach me was because I could not possibly imagine where the $20,000 would come from. So I simply held my thought steady and let the power of attraction find its own ways and means.

One day while walking on the street, taking deep breathing exercises, the thought came: "My mind is surely a center of Divine operation. If God fills all space, then God must be in my mind also; if I want this money to study with Troward that I may know the truth of Life, then both the money and the truth must be mine, though I am unable to feel or see the physical manifestations of either; still," I declared, "it must be mine."

While these reflections were going on in my mind, there seemed to come up from within me the thought: "I am all the substance there is." Then, from another channel in my brain the answer seemed to come, "Of course, that's it; everything must have its beginning in mind. The "I" the Idea, must be the only one and primary substance there is, and this means money as well as everything else." My mind accepted this idea, and immediately all the tension of mind and body was relaxed.

There was a feeling of absolute certainty of being in touch with all the power Life has to give. All thought of money, teacher, or even my own personality, vanished in the great wave of joy which swept over my entire being. I walked on and on with this feeling of joy steadily increasing and expanding until everything about me seemed aglow with resplendent light. Every person I passed was illuminated as I was. All consciousness of personality had disappeared, and in its place there came that great and almost overwhelming sense of joy and contentment.

That night when I made my picture of the twenty thousand dollars it was with an entirely changed aspect. On previous occasions, when making my mental picture, I had felt that I was waking up something within myself. This time there was no sensation of effort. I simply counted over the twenty thousand dollars. Then, in a most unexpected manner, from a source of which I had no consciousness at the time, there seemed to open a possible avenue through which the money might reach me.

At first it took great effort not to be excited. It all seemed so wonderful, so glorious to be in touch with supply. But had not Troward cautioned his readers to keep all excitement out of their minds in the first flush of realization of union with Infinite supply, and to treat this fact as a perfectly natural result that had been reached through our demand? This was even more difficult for me than it was to hold the thought that "all the substance there is, I am; I (idea) am the beginning of all form, visible or invisible."

Just as soon as there appeared a circumstance which indicated the direction through which the twenty thousand dollars might come, I not only made a supreme effort to regard the indicated direction calmly as the first sprout of the seed I had sown in the absolute, but left no stone unturned to follow up that direction by fulfilling my part. By so doing one circumstance seemed naturally to lead to another, until, step-by-step, my desired twenty thousand dollars was secured. To keep my mind poised and free from excitement was my greatest effort.

This first concrete fruition of my study of Mental Science as expounded by Troward's book had come by a careful following of the methods he had outlined. In this connection, therefore, I can offer to the reader no better gift than to quote Troward's book, "The Edinburgh Lectures," from which may be derived a complete idea of the line of action I was endeavoring to follow. In the chapter on Causes and Conditions he says: "To get good results we must properly understand our relation to the great impersonal power we are using. It is intelligent, and we are intelligent, and the two intelligences must co-operate.

We must not fly in the face of the Law expecting it to do for us what it can only do through us; and we must therefore use our intelligence with the knowledge that it is acting as the instrument of a greater intelligence; and because we have this knowledge we may and should cease from all anxiety as to the final result.

In actual practice we must first form the ideal conception of our object with the definite intention of impressing it upon the universal mind -it is this thought that takes such thought out of the region of mere casual fancies -and then affirm that our knowledge of the Law is sufficient reason for a calm expectation of a corresponding result, and that therefore all necessary conditions will come to us in due order. We can then turn to the affairs of our daily life with the calm assurance that the initial conditions are either there already or will soon come into view. If we do not at once see them, let us rest content with the knowledge that the spiritual prototype is already in existence and wait till some circumstance pointing in the desired direction begins to show itself.

It may be a very small circumstance, but it is the direction and not the magnitude that is to be taken into consideration. As soon as we see it we should regard it as the first sprouting of the seed sown in the Absolute, and do calmly, and without excitement, whatever the circumstances seem to require, and then later on we shall see that this doing will in turn lead to a further circumstance in the same direction, until we find ourselves conducted, step by step, to the accomplishment of our object.

In this way the understanding of the great principle of the Law of Supply will, by repeated experiences, deliver us more and more completely out of the region of anxious thought and toilsome labor and bring us into a new world where the useful employment of all our powers, whether mental or physical, will only be an unfolding of our individuality upon the lines of its own nature, and therefore a perpetual source of health and happiness; a sufficient inducement, surely, to the careful study of the laws governing the relation between the individual and the Universal Mind."

To my mind, then as now, this quotation outlines the core and center of the method and manner of approach necessary for coming in touch with Infinite supply. At least it, together with the previously quoted statement, "My mind is a center of Divine operation," etc., constituted the only apparent means of attracting to myself the twenty thousand dollars. My constant endeavor to get into the spirit of these statements, and to attract to myself this needed sum, was about six weeks, at the end of which time I had in my bank the required twenty thousand dollars. This could be made into a long story, giving all the details, but the facts, as already narrated, will give you a definite idea of the magnetic condition of my mind while the twenty thousand dollars was finding its way to me.

From Love and Marrage
by Elizabeth Towne
ISBN: 1-60459-004-1

All our goings and comings are due to the Law of Attraction. The Law of Attraction giveth, and it taketh away. *Blessed* is the Law. *Let* it work. And forget not that *all* things are due to its working.

This does not mean that the Law has no way of working *except* through the conventionalities of a people. Many times the attraction is to break away from the conventional. *The stronger attraction always wins*— whatever is, is *best* for *that time and place.*

"Tudor" says he "enters into the silence daily at a particular hour and enjoys the mental picture of how he desires to be."

His success all depends upon the *equity* in that picture; upon its truth to the law of being.

From Thoughts are Things
by Prentice Mulford
ISBN: 1-934451-20-7

When we form a plan for any business, any invention, any undertaking, we are making something of that unseen element, our thought, as real, though unseen, as any machine of iron or wood. That plan or thought begins, as soon as made, to draw to itself, in more unseen elements, power to carry itself out, power to materialize itself in physical or visible substance. When we dread a misfortune, or live in fear of any ill, or expect ill luck, we make also a construction of unseen element, thought,—which, by the same law of attraction, draws to it destructive, and to you damaging, forces or elements. Thus the law for success is also the law for misfortune, according as it is used; even as the force of a man's arm can save another from drowning, or strike a dagger to his heart. Of whatever possible thing we think, we are building, in unseen substance, a construction which will draw to us forces or elements to aid us or hurt us, according to the character of thought we think or put out.

If you expect to grow old, and keep ever in your mind an image or construction of yourself as old and decrepit, you will assuredly be so. You are then making yourself so.

If you make a plan in thought, in unseen element, for yourself, as helpless, and decrepit, such plan will draw to you of unseen thought-element that which will make you weak, helpless, and decrepit. If, on the contrary, you make for yourself a plan for being always healthy, active, and vigorous, and stick to that plan, and refuse to grow decrepit, and refuse to believe the legions ot people who will tell you that you must grow old, you will not grow old. It is because you think it must be so, as people tell you, that makes it so.

If you in your mind are ever building an ideal of yourself as strong, healthy, and vigorous, you are building to yourself of invisible element that which is ever drawing to you more of health, strength, and vigour. You can make of your mind a magnet to attract health or weakness. If you love to think of the strong things in Nature, of granite mountains and heaving billows and resistless tempests, you attract to you their elements of strength.

If you build yourself in health and strength today, and despond and give up such thinking or building tomorrow, you do not destroy what in spirit and of spirit you have built up. That amount of element so added to your spirit can never be lost but you do, for the time, in so desponding, that is, thinking weakness, stop the building of your health-structure; and although your spirit is so much the stronger for that addition of element, it may not be strong enough to give quickly to the body what you may have taken from it through such despondent thought.

Persistency in thinking health, in imagining or idealizing yourself as healthy, vigorous, and symmetrical, is the cornerstone of health and beauty. Of that which you think most, that you will be, and that you will have most of. You say "No." But your bed-ridden patient is not thinking, "I am strong;" he or she is thinking, "I am so weak." Your dyspeptic man or woman is not thinking, "I will have a strong stomach."

They are ever saying, "I can't digest anything;" and they can't, for that very reason. We are apt to nurse our maladies rather than nurse ourselves. We want our maladies petted and sympathized with, more than ourselves. When we have a bad cold, our very cough sometimes says to others, unconsciously, "I am this morning an object for your sympathy. I am so afflicted!" It is the cold, then, that is calling out for sympathy. Were the body treated rightly, your own mind and all the minds about you would say to that weak element in you, "Get out of that body!" and the silent force of a few minds so directed would drive that weakness out. It would leave as Satan did when the man of Nazareth imperiously ordered him. Colds and all other forms of disease are only forms of Satan, and thrive also by nursing. Vigour and health are catching also as well as the measles.

What would many grown-up people give for a limb or two limbs that had in them the spring and elasticity of those owned by a boy twelve years old; for two limbs that could climb trees, walk on rail fences, and run because they loved to run, and couldn't help running? If such limbs so full of life could be manufactured and sold, would there not be a demand for them by those stout ladies and gentlemen who get in and out of their carriages as if their bodies weighed a ton? Why is it that humanity resigns itself with scarcely a protest to the growing heaviness, sluggishness, and stiffness that comes even with middle age? I believe, however, we compromise with this inertia, and call it dignity. Of course a man and a father and a citizen and a voter and a pillar of the State—of inertia—shouldn't run and cut up and kick up like a boy, because he can't. Neither should a lady who has grown to the dignity of a waddle run as she did when a girl of twelve, because she can't, either. Actually we put on our infirmities as we would masks, and hobble around in them, saying, "This is the thing to do, because we can't do anything else." Sometimes we are even in a hurry to put them on; like the young gentleman who sticks an eye-glass to his eye, and thereby the sooner ruins the sight of a sound organ, in order to look tony or bookish.

There are more and more possibilities In Nature, in the elements, and in man and out of man; and they come as fast as man sees and knows how to use these forces in Nature and in himself. Possibilities and miracles mean the same thing.

The telephone sprung suddenly on "our folks" of two hundred years ago would have been a miracle, and might have consigned the person using it to the prison or the stake: all unusual manifestations of Nature's powers being then attributed to the Devil, because the people of that period had so much of the Devil, or cruder element, in them as to insist that the universe should not continually show and prove higher and higher expressions of the higher mind for man's comfort and pleasure.

From Practical Mental Influence
by William Walker Atkinson
ISBN: 1-60459-052-1

To quote a well-worn and much-used expression to illustrate this truth, "Like attracts Like," and "Birds of a Feather flock together." There is ever in operation this marvelous law of Attraction and Repulsion of Mental Energy— Persons allowing their thoughts to run along certain lines, and permitting the feelings to be expressed in certain ways, draw to themselves the Thought-Waves and mental influences of others keyed to the same mental key-note. And likewise they repel the waves and influences of an opposing nature. This is an important fact to remember in one's everyday life. Good attracts Good and repels Evil. Evil attracts Evil and repels Good. The predominant Mental Attitude serves to attract similar influences and to repel the opposing ones. Therefore watch carefully the character and nature of your thoughts — cultivate the desirable ones and repress the undesirable ones. Verily "As a man thinketh in his heart, so is he."

From Creative Mind
by Earnest Holmes
ISBN: 1-60459-072-6

As law works without variation, so does the law of attraction work the same way. All that we have to do is to drop the undesired thing from our thought, forgive ourselves and start anew. We must never even think of it again. Let go of it once and for all. Our various experiences will teach us more and more to try to mold all of our thoughts and desires, so that they will be in line with the fundamental purpose of the Great Mind, the expression of that which is perfect. To fear to make conscious use of the Law would be to paralyze all efforts of progress.

More and more will we come to see that a great cosmic plan is being worked out, and that all we have to do is to lend ourselves to it, in order that we may attain unto a real degree of life. As we do subject our thought to the greater purposes we are correspondingly blest, because we are working more in line with the Father, who from the beginning knew the end. We should never lose sight of the fact that we are each given the individual right to use the law, and that we cannot escape from using it.

Let us, then, go forward with the belief that a greater power is working through us; that all law is a law of good; that we have planted our seed of thought in the Mind of the Absolute; and that we can go our way rejoicing in the Divine privilege of working with the Infinite. There are many persons who are constantly unhappy because they seem always to be misunderstood. They find it hard to use the law of attraction in an affirmative way, and they keep on drawing to themselves experiences which they would rather have avoided. The trouble with them is that there is always an undercurrent of thought which either neutralizes or destroys whatever helpful thoughts they have set in motion in their moments of greater strength. Such persons are usually very sensitive, and while this is a quality which is most creative when under control, it is most destructive when uncontrolled, because it is most chaotic. They should first come to know the law and see how it works, and then treat themselves to overcome all sensitiveness. They should realize that everyone in the world is a friend, and prove this by never saying anything unkind to any one or about any one. They must within themselves see all people as perfect beings made in the Divine Image; and, seeing nothing else, they will in time be able to say that this is also the way that all people see them. Holding this as the law of their lives they will destroy all negative thought; and then, with that power which is always in a sensitive person, but which is now under control, they will find that life is theirs to do with as they please, the only requirement being that as they sow so must they also reap. We all know that anything that is unlike good is of short duration, but anything that embodies the good is like God, ever present and Eternal. We free ourselves through the same law under which we first bound ourselves.

The ordinary individual unknowingly does something that destroys any possibility of getting good results in the demonstration of prosperity. He affirms his good and makes his unity with it, and this is right, but he does not stop looking at it in others, which is wrong and is the cause of confusion. We cannot affirm a principle and deny it in the same breath. We must become what we want and we will never be able to do that while we still persist in seeing what we do not want, no matter where we see it. We cannot believe that something is possible for us without also believing the same for every individual.

One of the ways of attainment is, of a necessity, the way of universal love: coming to see all as the true sons of God, one with the Infinite Mind. This is no mere sentiment but the clear statement of a fundamental law and that man who does not obey it, is opposing the very thing that brought him into expression. It is true that through mental means alone he may bring to himself things and he may hold them as long as the will lasts. This is the ordinary way, but we want more than compelling things to appear. What we want is that things should gravitate to us because we are employing the same law that God uses. When we so attain this attitude of mind then that which is brought into manifestation will never be lost, for it will be as eternal as the law of God and cannot be destroyed forever. It is a comfort to know that we do not have to make things happen, but that the law of Divine love is all that we will ever need; it will relieve the overworked brain and the fagged muscle just to be still and know that we are One with the ALL in ALL.

How can we enter in, if at one and the same time we are believing for ourselves and beholding the beam in our brother's eye? Does that not obstruct the view and pervert our own natures? We must see only the good and let nothing else enter into our minds. Universal

love to all people and to all things is but returning love
to the source of all love, to Him who creates all in love
and holds all in divine care. The sun shines on all
alike. Shall we separate and divide where God has so
carefully united? We are dividing our own things when
we do this, and sooner or later the Law of Absolute
Justice that weighs out to each one his just measure
will balance the account, and then we shall be obliged
to suffer for the mistakes we have made. God does not
bring this agony on us but we have imposed it on
ourselves. If from selfish motives alone, we must love
all things and look upon all things as good, made from
the substance of the Father.

We can only hope to bring to ourselves that which we
draw through the avenue of love. We must watch our
thinking and if we have aught against any soul, get rid
of it as soon as possible. This is the only safe and sure
way. Did not Jesus at the supreme moment of sacrifice
ask that the Father forgive all the wrong that was
being clone to Him? Shall we suppose that 'we can do
it in a better way? If we do not at the present time love
all people, then we must learn how to do it, and the
way will become easier, when all condemnation is gone
forever and we behold only good. God is good and God
is Love; more than this we cannot ask nor conceive.

Another thing that we must eliminate is talking
about limitation; we must not even think of it or read
about it, or have any connection with it in any of our
thinking, for we get only that which we think, no more
and no less. This will be a hard thing to do. But if we
remember that we are working out the science of
being, though it may seem long and hard at times we
sooner or later do it, and once done it is done forever.
Every step in advance is an Eternal step, and will
never have to be taken again. We are not building for

a day or a year, but we are building for all time and for Eternity. So we will build the more stately mansion under the Supreme wisdom and the unfailing guidance of the Spirit, and we will do unto all, even as we would have them do unto us; there is no other way. The wise will listen, look and learn, then follow what they know to be the only way that is in line with the Divine will and purposes. So shall all see that God is good and in him is no evil.

From The Science of Getting Rich
by Wallace D. Wattles
ISBN: 1-934451-33-9

Thought is the only power which can produce
tangible riches from the Formless Substance. The stuff
from which all things are made is a substance which
thinks, and a thought of form in this substance
produces the form.
Original Substance moves according to its thoughts;
every form and process you see in nature is the visible
expression of a thought in Original Substance. As the
Formless Stuff thinks of a form, it takes that form; as
it thinks of a motion, it makes that motion. That is the
way all things were created. We live in a thought
world, which is part of a thought universe. The
thought of a moving universe extended throughout
Formless Substance, and the Thinking Stuff moving
according to that thought, took the form of systems of
planets, and maintains that form. Thinking Substance
takes the form of its thought, and moves according to
the thought. Holding the idea of a circling system of
suns and worlds, it takes the form of these bodies, and
moves them as it thinks. Thinking the form of a
slow-growing oak tree, it moves accordingly, and
produces the tree, though centuries may be required to
do the work. In creating, the Formless seems to move
according to the lines of motion it has established; the
thought of an oak tree does not cause the instant
formation of a full-grown tree, but it does start in
motion the forces which will produce the tree, along
established lines of growth.

From As a Man Thinketh
by James Allen
ISBN: 1-934451-39-8

Man's mind may be likened to a garden, which may be intelligently cultivated or allowed to run wild; but whether cultivated or neglected, it must, and will, *bring forth*. If no useful seeds are *put* into it, then an abundance of useless weed-seeds will *fall* therein, and will continue to produce their kind.

Just as a gardener cultivates his plot, keeping it free from weeds, and growing the flowers and fruits which he requires, so may a man tend the garden of his mind, weeding out all the wrong, useless, and impure thoughts, and cultivating toward perfection the flowers and fruits of right, useful, and pure thoughts. By pursuing this process, a man sooner or later discovers that he is the master-gardener of his soul, the director of his life. He also reveals, within himself, the laws of thought, and understands, with ever-increasing accuracy, how the thought-forces and mind elements operate in the shaping of his character, circumstances, and destiny.

Thought and character are one, and as character can only manifest and discover itself through environment and circumstance, the outer conditions of a person's life will always be found to be harmoniously related to his inner state. This does not mean that a man's circumstances at any given time are an indication of his *entire* character, but that those circumstances are so intimately connected with some vital thought-element within himself that, for the time being, they are indispensable to his development. Every man is where he is by the law of his being; the thoughts which he has built into his character have brought him there, and in the arrangement of his life there is no element of chance, but all is the result of a law which cannot err. This is just as true of those who feel "out of harmony" with their surroundings as of those who are contented with them.

As a progressive and evolving being, man is where he is that he may learn that he may grow; and as he learns the spiritual lesson which any circumstance contains for him, it passes away and gives place to other circumstances.

Man is buffeted by circumstances so long as he believes himself to be the creature of outside conditions, but when he realizes that he is a creative power, and that he may command the hidden soil and seeds of his being out of which circumstances grow, he then becomes the rightful master of himself.

That circumstances grow out of thought every man knows who has for any length of time practised self-control and self-purification, for he will have noticed that the alteration in his circumstances has been in exact ratio with his altered mental condition. So true is this that when a man earnestly applies himself to remedy the defects in his character, and makes swift and marked progress, he passes rapidly through a succession of vicissitudes.

The soul attracts that which it secretly harbours; that which it loves, and also that which it fears; it reaches the height of its cherished aspirations; it falls to the level of its unchastened desires,—and circumstances are the means by which the soul receives its own.

Every thought-seed sown or allowed to fall into the mind, and to take root there, produces its own, blossoming sooner or later into act, and bearing its own fruitage of opportunity and circumstance. Good thoughts bear good fruit, bad thoughts bad fruit.

The outer world of circumstance shapes itself to the inner world of thought, and both pleasant and unpleasant external conditions are factors, which make for the ultimate good of the individual. As the reaper of his own harvest, man learns both by suffering and bliss.

Following the inmost desires, aspirations, thoughts, by which he allows himself to be dominated, (pursuing the will-o'-the-wisps of impure imaginings or steadfastly walking the highway of strong and high endeavour), a man at last arrives at their fruition and fulfilment in the outer conditions of his life. The laws of growth and adjustment everywhere obtains.

A man does not come to the almshouse or the jail by the tyranny of fate or circumstance, but by the pathway of grovelling thoughts and base desires. Nor does a pure-minded man fall suddenly into crime by stress of any mere external force; the criminal thought had long been secretly fostered in the heart, and the hour of opportunity revealed its gathered power. Circumstance does not make the man; it reveals him to himself No such conditions can exist as descending into vice and its attendant sufferings apart from vicious inclinations, or ascending into virtue and its pure happiness without the continued cultivation of virtuous aspirations; and man, therefore, as the lord and master of thought, is the maker of himself the shaper and author of environment. Even at birth the soul comes to its own and through every step of its earthly pilgrimage it attracts those combinations of conditions which reveal itself, which are the reflections of its own purity and, impurity, its strength and weakness. Men do not attract that which they *want*, but that which they *are*. Their whims, fancies, and ambitions are thwarted at every step, but their inmost thoughts and desires are fed with their own food, be it foul or clean. The "divinity that shapes our ends" is in ourselves; it is our very self. Only himself manacles man: thought and action are the gaolers of Fate—they imprison, being base; they are also the angels of Freedom—they liberate, being noble. Not what he wishes and prays for does a man get, but what he justly earns. His wishes and prayers are only gratified and answered when they harmonize with his thoughts and actions.

In the light of this truth, what, then, is the meaning of "fighting against circumstances?" It means that a man is continually revolting against an *effect* without, while all the time he is nourishing and preserving its *cause* in his heart. That cause may take the form of a conscious vice or an unconscious weakness; but whatever it is, it stubbornly retards the efforts of its possessor, and thus calls aloud for remedy.

Men are anxious to improve their circumstances, but are unwilling to improve themselves; they therefore remain bound. The man who does not shrink from self-crucifixion can never fail to accomplish the object upon which his heart is set. This is as true of earthly as of heavenly things. Even the man whose sole object is to acquire wealth must be prepared to make great personal sacrifices before he can accomplish his object; and how much more so he who would realize a strong and well-poised life?

From In Tune With the Infinite
by Ralph Waldo Trine
ISBN: 1-60459-038-6

'The law of attraction works universally on every plane of action, and we attract whatever we desire or expect. If we desire one thing and expect another, we become like houses divided against themselves, which are quickly brought to desolation. Determine resolutely to expect only what you desire, then you will attract only what you wish for. . . . Carry any kind of thought you please about with you, and so long as you retain it, no matter how you roam over land or sea, you will unceasingly attract to yourself, knowingly or inadvertently, exactly and only what corresponds to your own dominant quality of thought. Thoughts are our private property, and we can regulate them to suit our taste entirely by steadily recognizing our ability so to do.'

We have just spoken of the drawing power of mind. Faith is nothing more nor less than the operation of the thought forces in the form of an earnest desire, coupled with expectation as to its fulfillment. And in the degree that faith, the earnest desire thus sent out, is continually held to and watered by firm expectation, in just that degree does it either draw to itself, or does it change from the unseen into the visible, from the spiritual into the material, that for which it is sent.

Let the element of doubt or fear enter in, and what would otherwise be a tremendous force will be so neutralized that it will fail of its realization. Continually held to and continually watered by firm expectation, it becomes a force, a drawing power, that is irresistible and absolute, and the results will be absolute in direct proportion as it is absolute.

We shall find, as we are so rapidly beginning to find today, that the great things said in regard to faith, the great promises made in connection with it, are not mere vague sentimentalities, but are all great scientific facts, and rest upon great immutable laws. Even in our very laboratory experiments we are beginning to discover the laws underlying and governing these forces. We are now beginning, some at least, to use them understandingly and not blindly, as has so often and so long been the case.

Much is said today in regard to the will. It is many times spoken of as if it were a force in itself. But will is a force, a power, only in so far as it is a particular form of the manifestation of the thought forces, for it is by what we call the 'will' that thought is focused and given a particular direction, and in the degree that thought is thus focused and given direction, is it effective in the work it is sent out to accomplish.

From Pushing to the Front
by Orison Swett Marden
ISBN: 1-60459-025-4

We were made for happiness, to express joy and gladness, to be prosperous. The trouble with us is that we do not trust the law of infinite supply, but close our natures so that abundance cannot flow to us. In other words, we do not obey the law of attraction. We keep our minds so pinched and our faith in ourselves so small, so narrow, that we strangle the inflow of supply. Abundance follows a law as strict as that of mathematics. If we obey it, we get the flow; if we strangle it, we cut it off. The trouble is not in the supply; there is abundance awaiting everyone on the globe.

Prosperity begins in the mind, and is impossible with a mental attitude which is hostile to it. We can not attract opulence mentally by a poverty-stricken attitude which is driving away what we long for. It is fatal to work for one thing and to expect something else. No matter how much one may long for prosperity, a miserable, poverty-stricken, mental attitude will close all the avenues to it. The weaving of the web is bound to follow the pattern. Opulence and prosperity can not come in through poverty-thought and failure-thought channels. They must be created mentally first. We must think prosperity before we can come to it.

How many take it for granted that there are plenty of good things in this world for others, comforts, luxuries, fine houses, good clothes, opportunity for travel, leisure, but not for them! They settle down into the conviction that these things do not belong to them, but are for those in a very different class. But why are you in a different class? Simply because you think yourself into another class; think yourself into inferiority; because you place limits for yourself. You put up bars between yourself and plenty. You cut off abundance, make the law of supply inoperative for you, by shutting your mind to it. *And by what law can you expect to get what you believe you can not get? By what philosophy can you obtain the good things of the world when you are thoroughly convinced that they are not for you?*

One of the greatest curses of the world is the belief in the necessity of poverty. Most people have a strong conviction that some must necessarily be poor; that they were made to be poor. But there was no poverty, no want, no lack, in the Creator's plan for man. There need not be a poor person on the planet. The earth is full of resources which we have scarcely yet touched. We have been poor in the very midst of abundance, simply because of our own blighting limiting thought.

We are discovering that thoughts are things, that they are incorporated into the life and form part of the character, and if we harbor the fear thought, the lack thought, if we are afraid of poverty, of coming to want, this poverty thought, fear thought incorporates itself in the very life texture and makes us the magnet to attract more poverty like itself.

It was not intended that we should have such a hard time getting a living, that we should just manage to squeeze along, to get together a few comforts, to spend about all of our time making a living instead of making a life. The life abundant, full, free, beautiful, was intended for us.

Let us put up a new image, a new ideal of plenty, of abundance. Have we not worshiped the God of poverty, of lack, of want, about long enough? Let us hold the thought that God is our great supply, that if we can keep in tune, in close touch with Him, so that we can feel our at-one-ness with Him, the great Source of all supply, abundance will flow to us and we shall never again know want.

There is nothing which the human race lacks so much as unquestioned, implicit confidence in the divine source of all supply. We ought to stand in the same relation to the Infinite Source as the child does to its parents. The child does not say, "I do not dare eat this food for fear that I may not get any more." It takes everything with absolute confidence and assurance that all its needs will be supplied, that there is plenty more where these things came from.

We do not have half good enough opinions of our possibilities; do not expect half enough of ourselves; we do not demand half enough, hence the meagerness, the stinginess of what we actually get. We do not demand the abundance which belongs to us, hence the leanness, the lack of fulness, the incompleteness of our lives. We do not demand royally enough. We are content with too little of the things worth while. *It was intended that we should live the abundant life*, that we should have plenty of everything that is good for us. No one was meant to live in poverty and wretchedness. *The lack of anything that is desirable is not natural to the constitution of any human being.*

Erase all the shadows, all the doubts and fears, and the suggestions of poverty and failure from your mind.

When you have become master of your thought, when you have once learned to dominate your mind, you will find that things will begin to come your way. Discouragement, fear, doubt, lack of self-confidence, are the germs which have killed the prosperity and happiness of tens of thousands of people. Every man must play the part of his ambition. If you are trying to be a successful man you must play the part. If you are trying to demonstrate opulence, you must play it, not weakly, but vigorously, grandly. You must feel opulent, you must think opulence, you must appear opulent. Your bearing must be filled with confidence. You must give the impression of your own assurance, that you are large enough to play your part and to play it superbly. Suppose the greatest actor living were to have a play written for him in which the leading part was to represent a man in the process of making a fortune—a great, vigorous, progressive character, who conquered by his very presence. Suppose this actor, in playing the part, were to dress like an unprosperous man, walk on the stage in a stooping, slouchy, slipshod manner, as though he had no ambition, no energy or life, as though he had no real faith that he could ever make money or be a success in business; suppose he went around the stage with an apologetic, shrinking, skulking manner, as much as to say, "Now, I do not believe that I can ever do this thing that I have attempted; it is too big for me. Other people have done it, but I never thought that I should ever be rich or prosperous. Somehow good things do not seem to be meant for me. I am just an ordinary man, I haven't had much experience and I haven't much confidence in myself, and it seems presumptuous for me to think I am ever going to be rich or have much influence in the world." What kind of an impression would he make upon the audience? Would he give confidence, would he radiate power or forcefulness, would he make people think that that kind of a weakling could create a fortune, could manipulate conditions which would produce money? Would not everybody say that the man was a failure? Would they not laugh at the idea of his conquering anything?

Poverty itself is not so bad as the poverty thought. It is the conviction that we are poor and must remain so that is fatal. It is the attitude of mind that is destructive, the facing toward poverty, and feeling so reconciled to it that one does not turn about face and struggle to get away from it with a determination which knows no retreat.

If we can conquer *inward poverty*, we can soon conquer poverty of outward things, for, when we change the mental attitude, the physical changes to correspond.

Holding the poverty thought, keeps us in touch with poverty-stricken, poverty-producing conditions; and the constant thinking of poverty, talking poverty, living poverty, makes us mentally poor. This is the worst kind of poverty.

We can not travel toward prosperity until the mental attitude faces prosperity. As long as we look toward despair, we shall never arrive at the harbor of delight.

The man who persists in holding his mental attitude toward poverty, or who is always thinking of his hard luck and failure to get on, can by no possibility go in the opposite direction, where the goal of prosperity lies.

There are multitudes of poor people in this country who are *half satisfied to remain in poverty*, and who have ceased to make a desperate struggle to rise out of it. They may work hard, but they have lost the hope, the expectation of getting an independence.

Many people keep themselves poor by fear of poverty, allowing themselves to dwell upon the possibility of coming to want, of not having enough to live upon, by allowing themselves to dwell upon conditions of poverty.

When you make up your mind that you are done with poverty forever; that you will have nothing more to do with it; that you are going to erase every trace of it from your dress, your personal appearance, your manner, your talk, your actions, your home; that you are going to show the world your real mettle; that you are no longer going to pass for a failure; that you have set your face persistently toward better things—a competence, an independence—and that nothing on earth can turn you from your resolution, you will be amazed to find what a reenforcing power will come to you, what an increase of confidence, reassurance, and self-respect.

Resolve with all the vigor you can muster that, since there are plenty of good things in the world for everybody, you are going to have your share, without injuring anybody else or keeping others back. It was intended that you should have a competence, an abundance. It is your birthright. You are success organized, and constructed for happiness, and you should resolve to reach your divine destiny.

From The Edinburgh and Dore
Lectures on Mental Science
by Thomas Troward
ISBN: 1-60459-067-X

The business of the will, then, is to retain the various faculties of our mind in that position where they are really doing the work we wish, and this position may be generalized into the three following attitudes; either we wish to act upon something, or be acted on by it, or to maintain a neutral position; in other words we either intend to project a force, or receive a force or keep a position of inactivity relatively to some particular object. Now the judgment determines which of these three positions we shall take up, the consciously active, the consciously receptive, or the consciously neutral; and then the function of the will is simply to maintain the position we have determined upon; and if we maintain any given mental attitude we may reckon with all certainty on the law of attraction drawing us to those correspondences which exteriorly symbolize the attitude in question. This is very different from the semi-animal screwing-up of the nervous forces which, with some people, stands for will-power. It implies no strain on the nervous system and is consequently not followed by any sense of exhaustion. The will-power, when transferred from the region of the lower mentality to the spiritual plane, becomes simply a calm and peaceful determination to retain a certain mental attitude in spite of all temptations to the contrary, knowing that by doing so the desired result will certainly appear.

The training of the will and its transference from the lower to the higher plane of our nature are among the first objects of Mental Science. The man is summed up in his will. Whatever he does by his own will is his own act; whatever he does without the consent of his will is not his own act but that of the power by which his will was coerced; but we must recognize that, on the mental plane, no other individuality can obtain control over our will unless we first allow it to do so; and it is for this reason that all legitimate use of Mental Science is towards the strengthening of the will, whether in ourselves or others, and bringing it under the control of an enlightened reason. When the will realizes its power to deal with first cause it is no longer necessary for the operator to state to himself *in extenso* all the philosophy of its action every time he wishes to use it, but, knowing that the trained will is a tremendous spiritual force acting on the plane of first cause, he simply expresses his desire with the intention of operating on that plane, and knows that the desire thus expressed will in due time externalize itself as concrete fact. He now sees that the point which really demands his earnest attention is not whether he possesses the power of externalizing any results he chooses, but of learning to choose wisely what results to produce. For let us not suppose that even the highest powers will take us out of the law of cause and effect. We can never set any cause in motion without calling forth those effects which it already contains in embryo and which will again become causes in their turn, thus producing a series which must continue to flow on until it is cut short by bringing into operation a cause of an opposite character to the one which originated it. Thus we shall find the field for the exercise of our intelligence continually expanding with the expansion of our powers; for, granted a good intention, we shall always wish to contemplate the results of our action as far as our intelligence will permit. We may not be able to see very far, but there is one safe general principle to be gained from what has already been said about causes and conditions, which is that the whole sequence always partakes of the same character as the initial cause: if that character is negative, that is, destitute of any desire to externalize kindness, cheerfulness, strength, beauty or some other sort of good, this negative quality will make itself felt all down the line; but if the opposite affirmative character is in the original motive, then it will reproduce its kind in forms of love, joy, strength and beauty with unerring precision. Before setting out, therefore, to produce new conditions by the exercise of our thought-power we should weigh carefully what further results they are likely to lead to; and here, again, we shall find an ample field for the training of our will, in learning to acquire that self-control which will enable us to postpone an inferior present satisfaction to a greater prospective good.

From The Power of Your Subconscious Mind
by Dr. Joseph Murphy
ISBN: 1-60459-048-3

Many years ago I met a young boy in Australia who wanted to become a physician and surgeon, but he had no money. I explained to him how a seed deposited in the soil attracts to itself everything necessary for its unfolding, and that all he had to do was to take a lesson from the seed and deposit the required idea in his subconscious mind. For expenses this young, brilliant boy used to clean out doctors' offices, wash windows, and do odd repair jobs. He told me that every night, as he went to sleep, he used to picture in his mind's eye a medical diploma on a wall with his name on it in big, bold letters. He used to clean and shine the framed diplomas in the medical building where he worked. It was not hard for him to engrave the image of a diploma in his mind and develop it there. Definite results followed as he persisted with his mental picture every night for about four months.

The sequel of this story was very interesting. One of the doctors took a great liking to this young boy and after training him in the art of sterilizing instruments, giving hypodermic injections, and other miscellaneous first aid work, he employed him as a technical assistant in his office. The doctor later sent him to medical school at his own expense. Today, this young man is a prominent medical doctor in Montreal,

Canada. He discovered the law of attraction by using his subconscious mind the right way. He operated an age old law, which says, "Having seen the end, you have willed the means to the realization of the end." The end in this case was to become a medical doctor.

This young man was able to imagine, see, and feel the reality of being a doctor. He lived with that idea, sustained it, nourished it, and loved it until through his imagination it penetrated the layers of his subconscious mind and became a conviction, thereby attracting to him everything necessary for the fulfillment of his dream.

From Mental Chemistry
by Charles F. Haanel
ISBN: 1-934451-32-0

Thought is the vital force or energy which is being developed and which has produced such startling results in the last half century, as to bring about a world which would be absolutely inconceivable to a man existing only 50 or even 25 years ago. If such results have been secured by organizing these mental powerhouses in 50 years, what may not be expected in another 50 years?

Some will say, if these principles are true, why are we not demonstrating them; as the fundamental principle is obviously correct, why do we not get proper results? We do; we get results in exact accordance with our understanding of the law and our ability to make the proper application. We did not secure results from the laws governing electricity until someone formulated the law and showed us how to apply it. Mental action inaugurates a series of vibrations in the ether, which is the substance from which all things proceed, which in their turn induce a corresponding grosser vibration in the molecular substance until finally mechanical action is produced.

This puts us in an entirely new relation to our environment, opening out possibilities hitherto undreamt of, and this by an orderly sequence of law which is naturally involved in our new mental attitude.

It is clear, therefore, that thoughts of abundance will respond only to similar thoughts; the wealth of the individual is seen to be what he inherently is. Affluence within is found to be the secret of attraction for affluence without. The ability to produce is found to be the real source of wealth of the individual. It is for this reason that he who has his heart in his work is certain to meet with unbounded success. He will give and continually give, and the more he gives the more he will receive.

Thought is the energy by which the law of attraction is brought into operation, which eventually manifests in abundance in the lives of men.

The source of all power, as of all weakness, is from within; the secret of all success as well as all failure is likewise from within. All growth is an unfoldment from within. This is evident from all Nature; every plant, every animal, every human is a living testimony to this great law, and the error of the ages is in looking for strength or power from without.

A thorough understanding of this great law which permeates the Universe leads to the acquirement of that state of mind which develops and unfolds a creative thought which will produce magical changes in life. Golden opportunities will be strewn across your path, and the power and perception to properly utilize them will spring up within you, friends will come unbidden, circumstances will ad just themselves to changed conditions; you will have found the "Pearl of greatest price."

Wisdom, strength, courage and harmonious conditions are the result of power, and we have seen that all power is from within; likewise every lack, limitation or adverse circumstance is the result of weakness, and weakness is simply absence of power; it comes from nowhere; it is nothing—the remedy, then is simply to develop power.

This is the key with which many are converting loss into gain, fear into courage, despair into joy, hope into fruition. This may seem to be too good to be true, but remember that within a few years, by the touch of a button or the turn of a lever, science has placed almost infinite resources at the disposal of man. Is it not possible that there are other laws containing still great possibilities?

Let us see what are the most powerful forces in Nature. In the mineral world everything is sold and fixed. In the animal and vegetable kingdom it is in a state of flux, forever changing, always being created and recreated. In the atmosphere we find heat, light and energy. Each realm becomes finer and more spiritual as we pass from the visible to the invisible, from the coarse to the fine, from the low potentiality to the high potentiality. When we reach the invisible we find energy in its purest and most volatile state.

And as the most powerful forces of Nature are the invisible forces, so we find that the most powerful forces of man are his invisible forces, his spiritual force, and the only way in which the spiritual force can manifest is through the process of thinking. Thinking is the only activity which the spirit possesses, and thought is the only product of thinking.

Addition and subtraction are therefore spiritual transactions; reasoning is a spiritual process; ideas are spiritual conceptions; questions are spiritual searchlights and logic, argument and philosophy are parts of the spiritual machinery.

Every thought brings into action certain physical tissue, parts of the brain, nerve or muscle. This produces an actual physical change in the construction of the tissue. Therefore it is only necessary to have a certain number of thoughts on a given subject in order to bring about a complete change in the physical organization of a man.

This is the process by which failure is changed to success. Thoughts of courage, power, inspiration, harmony, are substituted for thoughts of failure, despair, lack, limitation and discord, and as these thoughts take root, the physical tissue is changed and the individual sees life in a new light, old things have actually passed away; all things have become new; he is born again, this time born of the spirit; life has anew meaning for him; he is reconstructed and is filled with joy, confidence, hope, energy. He sees opportunities for success to which he was heretofore blind. He recognizes possibilities which before had no meaning for him. The thoughts of success with which he has been impregnated are radiated to those around him, and they in turn help him onward and upward; he attracts to him new and successful associates, and this in turn changes his environment; so that by this simple exercise of thought, a man changes not only himself, but his environment, circumstances and conditions.

You will see, you must see, that we are at the dawn of a new day; that the possibilities are so wonderful, so fascinating, so limitless as to be almost bewildering. A century ago any man with an aeroplane or even a Gattling gun could have annihilated a whole army equipped with the implements of warfare then in use. So it is at preset. Any man with a knowledge of the possibilities of modern metaphysics has an inconceivable advantage over the multitude.

Mind is creative and operates through the law of attraction. We are not to try to influence anyone to do what we think they should do. Each individual has a right to choose for himself, but aside from this we would be operating under the laws of force, which is destructive in its nature and just the opposite of the law of attraction. A little reflection will convince you that all the great laws of nature operate in silence and that the underlying principle is the law of attraction. It is only destructive processes, such as earthquakes and catastrophies, that employ force. Nothing good is ever accomplished in that way.

To be successful, attention must invariably be directed to the creative plane; it must never be competitive. You do not wish to take anything away from any one else; you want to create something for yourself, and what you want for yourself you are perfectly willing that every one else should have.

You know that it is not necessary to take from one to give to another, but that the supply for all is abundant. Nature's storehouse of wealth is inexhaustible and if there seems to be a lack of supply anywhere it is only because the channels of distribution are as yet imperfect.

Abundance depends upon a recognition of the laws of Abundance. Mind is not only the creator, but the only creator of all there is. Certainly nothing can be created before we know that it can be created and then make the proper effort. There is no more Electricity in the world today than there was fifty years ago, but until someone recognized the law by which it could be made of service, we received no benefit; now that the law is understood, practically the whole world is illuminated by it. So with the law of Abundance; it is only those who recognize the law and place themselves in harmony with it, who share in its benefits.

A recognition of the law of abundance develops certain mental and moral qualities, among which are Courage, Loyalty, Tact, Sagacity, Individuality and Constructiveness. These are all moods of thought, and as all thought is creative, they manifest in objective conditions corresponding with the mental condition. This is necessarily true because the ability of the individual to think is his ability to act upon the Universal Mind and bring it into manifestation; it is the process whereby the individual becomes a channel for the differentiation of the Universal. Every thought is a cause and every condition an effect.

This principle endows the individual with seemingly transcendental possibilities, among which is the mastery of conditions through the creation and recognition of opportunities. This creation of opportunity implies the existence or creation of the necessary qualities or talents which are thought forces and which result in a consciousness of power which future events cannot disturb. It is this organization of victory or success within the mind, this consciousness of power within, which constitutes the responsive harmonious action whereby we are related to the objects and purposes which we seek. This is the law of attraction in action; this law, being the common property of all, can be exercised by any one having sufficient knowledge of its operation.

Courage is the power of the mind which manifests in the love of mental conflict; it is a noble and lofty sentiment; it is equally fitted to command or obey; both require courage. It often has a tendency to conceal itself. There are men and women, too, who apparently exist only to do what is pleasing to others, but when the time comes and the latent will is revealed, we find under the velvet glove an iron hand, and no mistake about it. True courage is cool, calm, and collected, and is never foolhardy, quarrelsome, ill-natured or contentious.

Accumulation is the power to reserve and preserve a part of the supply which we are constantly receiving, so as to be in a position to take advantage of the larger opportunities which will come as soon as we are ready for them. Has it not been said, "To him that hath shall be given"? All successful business men have this quality, well developed. James J. Hill, who recently died, leaving an estate of over fifty-two million dollars said: "If you want to know whether you are destined to be a success or failure in life, you can easily find out. The test is simple and it is infallible: Are you able to save money? If not, drop out. You will lose. You may think not, but you will lose as sure as you live. The seed of success is not in you."

This is very good so far as it goes, but any one who knows the biography of James J. Hill knows that he acquired his fifty million dollars by following the exact methods we have given. In the first place, he started with nothing; he had to use his imagination to idealize the vast railroad which he projected across the western prairies. He then had to come into a recognition of the law of abundance in order to provide the ways and means for materializing it; unless he had followed out this program he would never had anything to save.

Accumulativeness acquires momentum; the more you accumulate the more you desire, and the more you desire the more you accumulate, so that it is but a short time until the action and reaction acquire a momentum that cannot be stopped. It must, however, never be confounded with selfishness, miserliness or penuriousness; they are perversions and will make any true progress impossible.

Constructiveness is the creative instinct of the mind. It will be readily seen that every successful business man must be able to plan, develop or construct. In the business world it is usually referred to as initiative. It is not enough to go along in the beaten path. New ideas must be developed, new ways of doing things. It manifests in building, designing, planning, inventing, discovering, improving. It is a most valuable quality and must be constantly encouraged and developed. Every individual possesses it in some degree, because he is a center of consciousness in that infinite and Eternal Energy from which all things proceed.

Water manifests on three planes, as ice, as water and as steam; it is all the same compound; the only difference is the temperature, but no one would try to drive an engine with ice; convert it into steam and it easily takes up the load. So with your energy; if you want it to act on the creative plane, you will have to begin by melting the ice with the fire of imagination, and you will find the stronger the fire, and the more ice you melt, the more powerful your thought will become, and the easier it will be for you to materialize your desire.

Sagacity is the ability to perceive and co-operate with Natural Law. True Sagacity avoids trickery and deceit as it would the leprosy; it is the product of that deep insight which enables on to penetrate into the heart of things and understand how to set causes in motion which will inevitably create successful conditions.

Tact is a very subtle and at the same time a very important factor in business success. It is very similar to intuition. To possess tact one must have a fine feeling, must instinctively know what to say or what to do. In order to be tactful one must possess Sympathy and Understanding, the understanding which is so rare, for all men see and hear and feel, but how desperately few "understand." Tact enables one to foresee what is about to happen and calculate the result of actions. Tact enables us to feel when we are in the presence of physical, mental and moral cleanliness, for these are today invariably demanded as the price of success.

Loyalty is one of the strongest links which bind men of strength and character. It is one which can never be broken with impunity. The man who would lose his right hand rather than betray a friend will never lack friends. The man who will stand in silent guard, until death, if need be, besides the shrine of confidence or friendship of those who have allowed him to enter will find himself linked with a current of cosmic power which will attract desirable conditions only. It is conceivable that such a person should ever meet with lack of any kind.

From The Secret of the Ages
by Robert Collier
ISBN: 1-934451-68-1

The old adage that "He profits most who serves best" is no mere altruism.

Look around you. What businesses are going ahead? What men are making the big successes? Are they the ones who grab the passing dollar, careless of what they offer in return? Or are they those who are striving always to give a little greater value, a little more work than they are paid for?

When scales are balanced evenly, a trifle of extra weight thrown into either side overbalances the other as effectively as a ton.

In the same way, a little better value, a little extra effort, makes the man or the business stand out from the great mass of mediocrity like a tall man among pigmies, and brings results out of all proportion to the additional effort involved.

It pays—not merely altruistically, but in good, hard, round dollars—to give a little more value than seems necessary, to work a bit harder than you are paid for. It's that extra ounce of value that counts.

For the law of attraction is service. We receive in proportion as we give out. In fact, we usually receive in far greater proportion. "Cast thy bread upon the waters and it will return to you an hundred-fold."

Back of everything is the immutable law of the Universe—that what you are but the effect. Your thoughts are the causes. The only way you can change the effect is by first changing the cause.

People live in poverty and want because they are so wrapped up in their sufferings that they give out thoughts only of lack and sorrow. They expect want. They open the door of their mind only to hardship and sickness and poverty. True—they hope for something better—but their hopes are so drowned by their fears that they never have a chance.

You cannot receive good while expecting evil. You cannot demonstrate plenty while looking for poverty. "Blessed is he that expecteth much, for verily his soul shall be filled." Solomon outlined the law when he said:

"There is that scattereth, and increaseth yet more;
And there is that withholdeth more than is meet, but it tendeth only to want.
The liberal soul shall be made fat;
And he that watereth shall be watered also himself."

The Universal Mind expresses itself largely through the individual. It is continually seeking an outlet. It is like a vast reservoir of water, constantly replenished by mountain springs. Cut a channel to it and the water will flow in ever-increasing volume. In the same way, if you once open up a channel of service by which the Universal Mind can express itself through you, its gifts will flow in ever increasing volume and *you* will be enriched in the process.

This is the idea through which great bankers are made. A foreign country needs millions for development. Its people are hard working, but lack the necessary implements to make their work productive. How are they to find the money?

They go to a banker—put their problem up to him. He has not the money himself, but he knows how and where to raise it. He sells the promise to pay of the foreign country (their bonds, in other words) to people who have money to invest. His is merely a service. But it is such an invaluable service that both sides are glad to pay him liberally for it.

In the same way, by opening up a channel between universal supply and human needs—by doing your neighbors or your friends or your customer's service—you are bound to profit yourself. And the wider you open your channel—the greater service you give or the better values you offer—the more things are bound to flow through your channel, the more you are going to profit thereby.

But you've got to *use* your talent if you want to profit from it. It matters not how small your service—using it will make it greater. You don't have to retire to a cell and pray. That is a selfish method—selfish concern for your own soul to the exclusion of all others. Mere self-denial or asceticism as such does no one good. You've got to DO something, to USE the talents God has given you to make the world better for your having been in it.

Remember the parable of the talents. You know what happened to the man who went off and hid his talent, whereas those who made use of theirs were given charge over many things.

That parable, it has always seemed to me, expresses the whole law of life. The only right is to use all the forces of good. The only wrong is to neglect or to abuse them.

"Thou shalt love the Lord thy God. This is the first and the greatest Commandment." Thou shalt show thy love by using to the best possible advantage the good things (the "talents" of the parable) that He has placed in your hands. "And the second is like unto it. Thou shalt love thy neighbor as thyself." Thou shalt not abuse the good things that have been provided you in such prodigality, by using them against your neighbor. Instead, thou shalt treat him (love him) as he would treat you. Thou shalt use the good about you for the advantage of all.

If you are a banker, you've got to use the money you have in order to make more money. If you are a merchant, you've got to sell the goods you have in order to buy more goods. If you are a doctor, you must help the patient you have in order to get more practice. If you are a clerk, you must do your work a little better than those around you if you want to earn more money than they. And if you want more of the universal supply, you must use that which you have in such a way as to make yourself of greater service to those around you.

"Whosoever shall be great among you," said Jesus, "shall be your minister, and whosoever of you will be the chiefest, shall be servant of all." In other words, if you would be great, you must serve. And he who serves most shall be greatest of all.

If you want to make more money, instead of seeking it for yourself, see how you can make more for others. In the process you will inevitably make more for yourself, too. We get as we give—but we must give first.

It matters not where you start—you may be a day laborer. But still you can give—give a bit more of energy, of work, of thought, than you are paid for. "Whosoever shall compel thee to go a mile," said Jesus, "go with him twain." Try to put a little extra skill into your work. Use your mind to find some better way of doing whatever task may be set for you. It won't be long before you are out of the common labor class.

There is no kind of work than cannot be bettered by thought. There is no method that cannot be improved by thought. So give generously of your thought to your work. Think every minute you are at it—"Isn't there some way in which this could be done easier, quicker, better?" Read in your spare time everything that relates to your own work or to the job ahead of you. In these days of magazines and books and libraries, few are the occupations that are not thoroughly covered in some good work.

Remember in Lorimer's "Letters of a Self-Made Merchant to His Son," the young fellow that old Gorgan Graham hired against

his better judgment and put in the "barrel gang" just to get rid of him quickly? Before the month was out the young fellow had thought himself out of that job by persuading the boss to get a machine that did the work at half the cost and with a third of the gang. Graham just had to raise his pay and put him higher up. But he wouldn't stay put. No matter what the job, he always found some way it could be done better and with fewer people, until he reached the top of the ladder.

There are plenty of men like that in actual life. They won't stay down. They are as full of bounce as a cat with a small boy and a dog after it. Thrown to the dog from an upper window, it is using the time of falling to get set for the next jump. By the time the dog leaps for where it hit, the cat is up the tree across the street.

The true spirit of business is the spirit of that plucky old Danish sea captain, Peter Tordenskjold. Attacked by a Swedish frigate, after all his crew but one had been killed and his supply of cannon balls was exhausted, Peter boldly kept up the fight, firing pewter dinner-plates and mugs from his one remaining gun.

One of the pewter mugs hit the Swedish captain and killed him, and Peter sailed off triumphant!

Look around *you* now. How can *you* give greater value for what you get? How can you *serve* better? How can you make more money for your employers or save more for your customers? Keep that thought ever in the forefront of your mind and you'll never need to worry about making more for yourself!

From The Power of Concentration
by Theron Q. Dumont
(William Walker Atkinson)
ISBN: 1-60459-051-3

You will find that each day as you focus your forces on this thought at the center of the stream of consciousness, new plans, ideas and methods will flash into your mind. There is a law of attraction that will help you accomplish your purpose. An advertiser, for instance, gets to thinking along a certain line. He has formed his own ideas, but he wants to know what others think. He starts out to seek ideas and he soon finds plenty of books, plans, designs, etc., on the subject, although when he started he was not aware of their existence.

The same thing is true in all lines. We can attract those things that will help us. Very often we seem to receive help in a miraculous way. It may be slow in coming, but once the silent unseen forces are put into operation, they will bring results so long as we do our part. They are ever present and ready to aid those who care to use them. By forming a strong mental image of your desire, you plant the thought-seed which begins working in your interest and, in time, that desire, if in harmony with your higher nature, will materialize.

It may seem that it would be unnecessary to caution you to concentrate only upon achievement that will be good for you and work no harm to another, but there are many who forget others and their rights, in their

anxiety to achieve success. All good things are possible
for you to have, but only as you bring your forces into
harmony with that law that requires that we mete out
justice to fellow travelers as we journey along life's
road. So first think over the thing wanted and if it
would be good for you to have; say, "I want to do this;
I am going to work to secure it. The way will be open
for me."

If you fully grasp mentally the thought of success
and hold it in mind each day, you gradually make a
pattern or mold which in time will materialize. But by
all means keep free from doubt and fear, the
destructive forces. Never allow these to become
associated with your thoughts.

At last you will create the desired conditions and
receive help in many unlooked-for ways that will lift
you out of the undesired environment. Life will then
seem very different to you, for you will have found
happiness through awakening within yourself the
power to become the master of circumstances instead
of their slave.

To the beginner in this line of thought some of the
things stated in this book may sound strange, even
absurd, but, instead of condemning them, give them a
trial. You will find they will work out.

The inventor has to work out his idea mentally
before he produces it materially. The architect first
sees the mental picture of the house he is to plan and
from this works out the one we see. Every object, every
enterprise, must first be mentally created.

I know a man that started in business with thirteen
cents and not a dollar's worth of credit. In ten years he
has built up a large and profitable business. He
attributes his success to two things—belief that he
would succeed and hard work. There were times when

it did not look like he could weather the storm. He was being pressed by his creditors who considered him bankrupt. They would have taken fifty cents on the dollar for his notes and considered themselves lucky. But by keeping up a bold front he got an extension of time when needed. When absolutely necessary for him to raise a certain sum at a certain time he always did it. When he had heavy bills to meet he would make up his mind that certain people that owed him would pay by a certain date and they always did. Sometimes he would not receive their check until the last mail of the day of the extension, and I have known him to send out a check with the prospect of receiving a check from one of his customers the following day. He would have no reason other than his belief in the power of affecting the mind of another by concentration of thought for expecting that check, but rarely has he been disappointed.

Just put forth the necessary concentrated effort and you will be wonderfully helped from sources unknown to you.

From Think and Grow Rich
by Napoleon Hill
ISBN: 1-934451-35-5

First. I know that I have the ability to achieve the object of my Definite Purpose in life, therefore, I demand of myself persistent, continuous action toward its attainment, and I here and now promise to render such action.

Second. I realize the dominating thoughts of my mind will eventually reproduce themselves in outward, physical action, and gradually transform themselves into physical reality, therefore, I will concentrate my thoughts for thirty minutes daily, upon the task of thinking of the person I intend to become, thereby creating in my mind a clear mental picture of that person.

Third. I know through the principle of auto-suggestion, any desire that I persistently hold in my mind will eventually seek expression through some practical means of attaining the object back of it, therefore, I will devote ten minutes daily to demanding of myself the development of *self-confidence*.

Fourth. I have clearly written down a description of my *definite chief aim* in life, and I will never stop trying, until I shall have developed sufficient self-confidence for its attainment.

Fifth. I fully realize that no wealth or position can long endure, unless built upon truth and justice, therefore, I will engage in no transaction which does not benefit all whom it affects. I will succeed by attracting to myself the forces I wish to use, and the cooperation of other people. I will induce others to serve me, because of my willingness to serve others. I will eliminate hatred, envy, jealousy, selfishness, and cynicism, by developing love for all humanity, because I know that a negative attitude toward others can never bring me success. I will cause others to believe in me, because I will believe in them, and in myself.

I will sign my name to this formula, commit it to memory, and repeat it aloud once a day, with full *faith* that it will gradually influence my *thoughts* and *actions* so that I will become a self-reliant, and successful person.

Back of this formula is a law of Nature which no man has yet been able to explain. It has baffled the scientists of all ages. The psychologists have named this law "auto-suggestion," and let it go at that.

The name by which one calls this law is of little importance. The important fact about it is— it works for the glory and success of mankind, *if* it is used constructively. On the other hand, if used destructively, it will destroy just as readily. In this statement may be found a very significant truth, namely; that those who go down in defeat, and end their lives in poverty, misery, and distress, do so because of negative application of the principle of auto-suggestion. The cause may be found in the fact that *all impulses of thought have a tendency to clothe themselves in their physical equivalent.*

The subconscious mind, (the chemical laboratory in which all thought impulses are combined, and made ready for translation into physical reality), makes no distinction between constructive and destructive thought impulses. It works with the material we feed it, through our thought impulses. The subconscious mind will translate into reality a thought driven by *fear* just as readily as it will translate into reality a thought driven by *courage*, or *faith*.

From Thoughts I Met On the Highway
by Ralph Waldo Trine
ISBN: 1-60459-047-5

In one of those valuable essays of Prentice Mulford entitled "Who Are Our Relations?" he points us to the fact, and with so much insight and common sense, that our relations are not always or necessarily those related to us by blood ties, those of our immediate households, but those most nearly allied to us in mind and in spirit, many times those we have never seen, but that we shall sometime, somewhere be drawn to through the ceaselessly working Law of Attraction, whose basis is that like attracts like. And so in staying too closely with the accustomed relations we may miss the knowledge and the companionship of those equally or even more closely related.

We need these changes to get the kinks out of our minds, our nerves, our muscles—the cobwebs off our faces. We need them to whet again the edge of appetite. We need them to invite the mind and the soul to new possibilities and powers. We need them in order to come back with new implements, or with implements redressed, sharpened, for the daily duties. It is like the chopper working too long with axe unground. There comes the time when an hour at the stone will give it such persuasive power that he can chop and cord in the day what he otherwise would in two or more, and with far greater ease and satisfaction.

We need periods of being by ourselves — alone. Sometimes a fortnight or even a week will do wonders for one, unless he or she has drawn too heavily upon the account. The simple custom, moreover, of taking an hour, or even a half hour, alone in the quiet, in the midst of the daily routine of life, would be the source of inestimable gain for countless numbers.

If such changes can be in closer contact with the fields and with the flowers that are in them, the stars and the sea that lies open beneath them, the woods and the wild things that are of them, one cannot help but find himself growing in love for and an ever fuller appreciation of these, and being at the same time so remade and unfolded that his love, his care, and his consideration for all mankind and for every living creature, will be the greater.

From Life Power and How To Use It
by Elizabeth Towne
ISBN: 1-60459-002-5

The Rev. R. F. Horton tells a little story of a remarkable answer to prayer.

He was with a party of tourists in Norway. In exploring some wild and marshy country one of the ladies lost one of her "goloshes." The overshoe could not be replaced short of Bergen, at the end of their tour, and it was out of the question to attempt to explore that wild country without rubbers. The golosh must be found, or the tour curtailed.

As you may imagine, every member of the party set diligently to work to find the missing rubber. Over and over they hunted the miles of glades and mountain sides they had traversed At last they gave it up and returned to the hotel.

But in the afternoon a thought came to Dr. Horton—why not pray that they find the shoe? So he prayed. And they rowed back up the fjord to the landing of the morning, and he got out and walked directly to the overshoe, in a spot he would have sworn he had before searched repeatedly.

I remember a similar experience of my own. There were four of us riding bicycles along a rather sandy road some distance from town. Two were spinning along on a tandem some distance ahead of us, on a down grade, when a rivet flew out and the chain dropped. The tandem ran for a quarter of a mile on down the hill and slowed up on the rise beyond, so that our friends were able to dismount without injury.

By this time we had overtaken them, having ridden in their track, and learned for the first time the cause of their halt. Of course everybody's immediate thought was, "Oh, we can never find that tiny gray rivet in this gray dust—probably the other bicycles ran over it—and home is three miles off!" But we all retraced our steps, diligently searching.

Two of the party are crack shots with the rifle, with very quick eyesight. I thought one of these two might find the rivet. But we all walked slowly back, far beyond the point where they became conscious of their loss, and no one spied the rivet.

Then it occurred to me that the high spirit within had not been called to our assistance. Immediately I said to myself, "Spirit, you know where the rivet is!—please show it to me!"

I thought of the spirit as the Law of Love or Attraction, which is the principle of all creation, and instantly the idea came that the little rivet could attract the eye's attention if the eye were willing to be attracted. These words floated into my mind, "Rivet, rivet, rivet my eye!"

By this time I had fallen behind the others. So I walked leisurely, calmly along, eyes willing, and those words saying themselves over and over in my mind.

And the rivet riveted my eye! I, who considered myself very slow of sight, found the rivet. And I know it was because I turned to the universal self, to God, to the Law of Attraction for the help needed, for the knowledge which not one of us had in consciousness, but which was certainly present in the universal mind in which we live and move and have our being.

Just the other day I had a little experience which illustrates the "man's extremity is God's opportunity" idea. For years I have said I could never find ready made garments to fit me. Have tried many times; waists all too short and narrow in front, sleeves skimpy. But I keep trying, every year; for everything is evolving you know, even clothes and tailors.

I wanted a new white lawn shirt waist and wondered if I couldn't find one ready made. I tried the biggest suit house in Springfield; no good.

Then one day I had an impulse to try the best places in Holyoke. I found one or two "almosts," but nothing that would quite do. So I gave it up.

Then I had another impulse to try a store of which I have always said, "I never found there anything I wanted." I nearly passed the store, saying to myself, "No use to try there, and it is late anyway." But there came the thought, or rather impression, that the spirit impelled me and I would better go.

"We'll see if it is the spirit," I said to myself—"I believe it is." It was. I found the [shirt] waist I wanted, and I found a pretty white lawn suit besides! And it was found in the most unlikely corner in the vicinity, according to my judgment and experience.

There is a little law in here that I want you to notice. The spirit leads us through impressions or attractions; and it is limited in its revelations by our mental makeup, which is the conscious and ruling part of us.

Why did not the spirit impress me in the first place to go to that store, where that [shirt] waist and dress had been waiting for me since spring? And I had wanted them since spring. The spirit did impress me about it, but when the spirit said "shirt waist" to me I said, "Springfield—if they haven't a fit there they won't have it anywhere; and anyway I know I'll never find it." But I tried—without faith. That shut the spirit up for the time.

But at the very first opportunity, on the first afternoon when I wasn't too busy to even think about such things, the spirit whispered "shirt waist" to me again. And I didn't let the spirit get any farther with its impressions; instead of asking the spirit where to go for a shirt waist I said, "Oh, yes, shirt waist—of course—I'll go to A.'s and B.'s and C.'s, where I generally get other things that suit me."

You see, my habit mind, preconceived opinions, again settled the matter. It was not until I had given up finding anything at these places, and was going right by the door of the other store, that the spirit had a chance even to whisper its name to me. The spirit had to lead me around all my prejudices in the matter, before it could get me to think of that place.

My mind was open to the thought of the shirt waist, but it was closed hard and fast against the idea of that particular store. At least the direct mental route to that store was closed. So the spirit had to lead me around by back-alley brain connections. But now the direct route is open.

The spirit always goes shopping with me, and nearly always the direct mental routes are open, so I have lots of fun shopping, never waste a lot of time at it, and I nearly always get just what I want, many times at bargain prices, though I almost never look at bargain ads in the papers. But many, many times have I gone into a store to buy a certain thing and found a big special sale on, of that very item.

Do you think these are very trivial things to be bothering the spirit about? I don't. The spirit is all-wise, all-powerful, everywhere present, and its chief end and joy is to direct folks aright.

The spirit is a sort of universal floor-walker to straighten out the snarls between supply and demand in all departments of life. And I think it is a pretty heedless or foolish individual who won't consult it in every little dilemma.

And I notice that, in spite of this thought, I find myself ignoring the spirit—thinking I know of course where I'd better go for a shirt waist.

It seems hard to remember that Life's store is always growing and changing, so that we can always save time, money and needless meandering, by asking the spirit.

Herein lies the secret of all our little experiences when it looks as if our leading of the spirit was all wrong and our prayers, longing and desires all unanswered: The spirit never fails us. It is we who grow weary following the spirit; which must lead us to the desired goal by way of our own mental paths.

You see, it is a matter of cutting new streets in our mental domain, so it won't be necessary for the spirit to take us by such roundabout ways. It is a matter of clearing out our rocky prejudices so we'll not have to travel around them.

And here the spirit helps us again. As soon as the spirit succeeded in getting me around all my prejudices and into that store I wiped away the prejudice. So there is a straight mental street now where none existed before. The next time the spirit says "shirt waist," to me it can send me straight to D.'s if it wants to.

Yes, the spirit "moves in a mysterious way its wonders to perform." It looks mysterious to us until we are led back by the straight way. Then it is so simple, so easy, we can hardly believe the spirit would condescend to it!

Ah, but it does! Nothing is too small, or too great, for the spirit's attention—if we believe. When we don't believe we are to be pitied—and the spirit keeps discreetly mum.

From Byways to Blessedness
by James Allen
ISBN: 1-934451-41-X

Revenge is a virus which eats into the very vitals of the mind, and poisons the entire spiritual being. Resentment is a mental fever which burns up the wholesome energies of the mind, and "taking offence" is a form of moral sickness which saps the healthy flow of kindliness and good-will, and from which men and women should seek to be delivered. The unforgiving and resentful spirit is a source of great suffering and sorrow, and he who harbors and encourages it, who does not overcome and abandon it, forfeits much blessedness, and does not obtain any measure of true enlightenment. To be hard-hearted is to suffer, is to be deprived of light and comfort; to be tender-hearted is to be serenely glad, is to receive light and be well comforted. It will seem strange to many to be told that the hard-hearted and unforgiving suffer most; yet it is profoundly true, for not only do they, by the law of attraction, draw to themselves the revengeful passions in other people, but their hardness of heart itself is a continual source of suffering. Every time a man hardens his heart against a fellow-being he inflicts upon himself five kinds of suffering— namely, the suffering of loss of love; the suffering of lost communion and fellowship; the suffering of a troubled and confused mind; the suffering of wounded passion or pride; and the suffering of punishment inflicted by others. Every act of unforgiveness entails upon the doer of that act these five sufferings; whereas every act of forgiveness brings to the doer five kinds of blessedness— the blessedness of love; the blessedness of increased communion and fellowship; the blessedness of a calm and peaceful mind; the blessedness of passion stilled and pride overcome; and the blessedness and kindness and good-will bestowed by others.

Numbers of people are today suffering the fiery torments of an unforgiving spirit, and only when they make an effort to overcome that spirit can they know what a cruel and exacting taskmaster they are serving. Only those who have abandoned the service of such a master for that of the nobler master of forgiveness can realize and know how grievous a service is the one, how sweet the other.

Let a man contemplate the strife of the world: how individuals and communities, neighbors and nations, live in continual retaliations towards each other; let him realize the heartaches, the bitter tears, the grievous partings and misunderstandings— yea, even the blood-shed and woe which spring from that strife— and, thus realizing, he will never again yield to ignoble thoughts of resentment, never again take offence at the actions of others, never again live in unforgiveness towards any being.

"Have good-will
To all that lives, letting unkindness die
And greed and wrath; so that your lives be made
Like soft airs passing by."

When a man abandons retaliation for forgiveness he passes from darkness to light. So dark and ignorant is unforgiveness that no being who is at all wise or enlightened could descend to it; but its darkness is not understood and known until it is left behind, and the better and nobler course of conduct is sought and practiced. Man is blinded and deluded only by his own dark and sinful tendencies; and the giving up of all unforgiveness means the giving up of pride and certain forms of passion, the abandonment of the deeply-rooted idea of the importance of one-self and of the necessity for protecting and defending that self; and when that is done the higher life, greater wisdom, and pure enlightenment, which pride and passion completely obscured, are revealed in all their light and beauty.

From The Law of Attraction
by William Walker Atkinson
ISBN: 1-60459-053-X

There are many people who seem to think that the only way in which the Law of Attraction operates is when one wishes hard, strong and steady. They do not seem to realize that a strong belief is as efficacious as a strong wish. The successful man believes in himself and his ultimate success, and, paying no attention to little setbacks, stumbles, tumbles and slips, presses on eagerly to the goal, believing all the time that he will get there. His views and aims may alter as he progresses, and he may change his plans or have them changed for him, but all the time he knows in his heart that he will eventually "get there." He is not steadily wishing he may get there — he simply feels and believes it, and thereby sets to operation the strongest forces known in the world of thought.

The man who just as steadily believes he is going to fail will invariably fail. How could he help it? There is no special miracle about it. Everything he does, thinks and says is tinctured with the thought of failure. Other people catch his spirit, and fail to trust him or his ability, which occurrences he in turn sets down as but other exhibitions of his ill luck, instead of ascribing them to his belief and expectation of failure. He is suggesting failure to himself all the time, and he invariably takes on the effect of the autosuggestion. Then, again, he by his negative thoughts shuts up that portion of his mind from which should come the ideas and plans conducive to success and which do come to the man who is expecting success because he believes in it. A state of discouragement is not the one in which bright ideas come to us. It is only when we are enthused and hopeful that our minds work out the bright ideas which we may turn to account.

Men instinctively feel the atmosphere of failure hovering around certain of their fellows, and on the other hand recognize something about others which leads them to say, when they hear of a temporary mishap befalling such a one: "Oh, he'll come out all right somehow — you can't down him." It is the atmosphere caused by the prevailing Mental Attitude. Clear up your Mental Atmosphere!

There is no such thing as chance. Law maintains everywhere, and all that happens because of the operation of Law. You cannot name the simplest thing that ever occurred by chance — try it, and then run the thing down to a final analysis, and you will see it as the result of law. It is as plain as mathematics. Plan and purpose; cause and effect. From the movements of worlds to the growth of the grain of mustard seed — all the result of Law. The fall of the stone down the mountainside is not chance — forces which had been in operation for centuries caused it. And back of that cause were other causes, and so on until the Causeless Cause is reached.

And Life is not the result of chance — the Law is here, too. The Law is in full operation whether you know it or not — whether you believe in it or not. You may be the ignorant object upon   which the Law operates, and bring yourself all sorts of trouble because of your ignorance of or opposition to the Law. Or you may fall in with the operations to the Law —

get into its current, as it were — and Life will seem a far different thing to you. You cannot get outside of the Law,   by refusing to have anything to do with it. You are at liberty to oppose it and produce all the friction you wish to — it doesn't' hurt the Law, and you may keep it up until you learn your lesson.

The Law of Thought Attraction is one name for the law, or rather for one manifestation of it. Again I say, your thoughts are real things. They go forth from you in all directions, combining with thoughts of like kind — opposing thoughts of a different character — forming combinations — going where they are attracted — flying away from thought centers opposing them. And your mind attracts the thought of others, which have been sent out by them conscious or unconsciously. But it attracts only those thoughts which are in harmony with its own. Like attracts like, and opposites repel opposites, in the world of thought.

If you set your mind to the keynote of courage, confidence, strength and success, you attract to yourself thoughts of like nature; people of like nature; things that fit in the mental tune. Your prevailing thought or mood determines that which is to be drawn toward you — picks out your mental bedfellow. You are today setting into motion thought currents which will in time attract toward you thoughts, people and conditions in harmony with the predominant note of your thought. Your thought will mingle with that of others of like nature and mind, and you will be attracted toward each other, and will surely come together with a common purpose sooner or later, unless one or the other of you should change the current of his thoughts.

Fall in with the operations of the law. Make it a part of yourself. Get into its currents. Maintain your poise.

Set your mind to the keynote of Courage, Confidence and Success. Get in touch with all the thoughts of that kind that are emanating every hour from hundreds of minds. Get the best that is to be had in the thought world. The best is there, so be satisfied with nothing less. Get into partnership with good minds. Get into the right vibrations. You must be tired of being tossed about by the operations of the Law — get into harmony with it.

From Science of Mind
by Earnest Holmes
ISBN: 1-60459-074-2

When we realize that as we deal with our own individuality we are dealing with Self-Conscious Mind, and when we realize that as we deal with subjective mind we are dealing with the Universal Subjectivity, we see at once that we have at our disposal a Power compared to which the united intelligence of the human race is as nothing; because the Universal Subjective Mind, being entirely receptive to our thought, is compelled by reason of Its very being to accept that thought and act upon it, no matter what the thought is. Since we are dealing with an Infinite Power, which knows only Its own ability to do, and since It can objectify any idea impressed upon It, there can be no limit to what It could or would do for us, other than the limit of our mental concept. Limitation could not be in Principle or in Law but only in the individual use that we make of It. Our individual use of It can only equal our individual capacity to understand It, to embody It. We cannot demonstrate beyond our ability to mentally conceive, or to mentally provide, an equivalent. We must have a mental equivalent of the thing we want, in order to demonstrate.

Subjectivity is entirely receptive and neutral, as we have learned, and It can take our thoughts only the way we think them. There is no alternative. If I say, "I am poor," and keep on saying, "I am poor," subconscious mind at once says, "Yes, you are poor." and keeps me poor, as long as I say it. This is all there is to poverty. It comes from impoverished thinking. We deal only with thoughts, for thoughts are things, and if the thought is right the condition will be right. An active thought will produce an active condition. Suppose I have thought poverty year after year, I have created a law, which keeps on perpetuating this condition. If the thought be unerased, the condition will remain. A law has been set in motion which says, "I am poor," and sees to it that it is so. This is, at first, auto-suggestion; then it becomes an unconscious memory, working day and night. This is what decides the law of attraction, because the laws of attraction and repulsion are entirely subjective. They may be conscious to start with, but they are subconscious as soon as they are set in motion. Now suppose I did not say I was poor, but came into the world with an unconscious thought of poverty; so long as that thought operated, I would be poor. I might not have understood the Law, but it would have been working all the time.

There is also a race-suggestion which says that some people are rich and some are poor; so we are all born or come into this world with a subjective tendency toward negative conditions. But we are also dealing with a subjective tendency toward ultimate good; because, in spite of all conditions, the race believes more in the good than in the evil; otherwise, it would not exist. It believes that everything will come out all right, rather than all wrong. This is the eternal hope and sense of all life.

No matter what may be in the soul, or subjective state of our thought, the conscious state can change it.

This is what treatment does. How can this be done? Through the most direct method imaginable—by consciously knowing that there is no subjective state of poverty, no inherited tendency toward limitation, no race-suggestion operating through subjectivity; nothing in, around or through it that believes in or accepts limitation in any way, shape, form or manner. The conscious state must now provide a higher form of thought. What does it do? It supplies a spiritual realization, a self-conscious realization, and says, "I partake of the nature and bounty of the All Good and I am now surrounded by everything whichmakes life worth while." What happens then? This Soul side of life, this Universal Medium, at once changes Its thought (because Its thought is deductive only) and says, "Yes, you are all of these things." Whatever is held in consciousness until it becomes a part of the subjective side of thought must take place in the world of affairs. Nothing can stop it. The reason we do not demonstrate more easily is that the objective state of our thought is too often neutralized by the subjective state. There is more fear of poverty than there is belief in riches. As long as that fear remains it is sure to produce a limited condition. Whatever is subjective must objectify. Matter is immaterial, unknowing, unthinking, and plastic in the hands of Law or Mind; and Law or Subjective Mind, which is entirely unvolitional, but not unintelligent, is compelled by its own subjectivity to receive the thought of the conscious mind, which alone can choose and decide. It follows then that whatever the conscious mind holds long enough is bound to be produced in external affairs; nothing can stop it, because we are dealing with Universal Law. This is called Divine Principle. It is the Medium in which we all live, move and have our being on the subjective side of life; our atmosphere in Universal Subjectivity; the medium through which all intercommunication takes place on every plane.

It follows from what we have said that any suggestion held in Creative Mind would produce its logical result, no matter what that suggestion might be. If it were a suggestion of destruction, it would destroy; for this is a neutral field. If it were a suggestion of good, it would construct.

From The Master Key To This Mystical Life Of Ours by Ralph Waldo Trine
ISBN: 1-60459-044-0

If one hold himself in the thought of poverty, he will be poor, and the chances are that he will remain in poverty. If he hold himself, whatever present conditions may be, continually in the thought of prosperity, he sets into operation forces that will sooner or later bring him into prosperous conditions. The law of attraction works unceasingly throughout the universe, and the one great and never changing fact in connection with it is, as we have found, that like attracts like. If we are one with this Infinite Power, this source of all things, then in the degree that we live in the realization of this oneness, in that degree do we actualize in our selves a power that will bring to us an abundance of all things that it is desirable for us to have. In this way we come into possession of a power where by we can actualize at all times those conditions that we desire.

As all truth exists now, and awaits simply our perception of it, so all things necessary for present needs exist now, and await simply the power in us to appropriate them. God holds all things in His hands. His constant word is, My child, acknowledge me in all your ways, and in the degree that you do this, in the degree that you live this, then what is mine is yours. Jehovah-jireh, — the Lord will provide. "He giveth to all men liberally and upbraideth not." He giveth liberally to all men who put themselves in the right attitude to receive from Him. He forces no good things upon anyone.

The old and somewhat prevalent idea of godliness and poverty has absolutely no basis for its existence, and the sooner we get away from it the better. It had its birth in the same way that the idea of asceticism came into existence, when the idea prevailed that there was necessarily a warfare between the flesh and the spirit. It had its origin therefore in the minds of those who had a distorted, a one-sided view of life. True godliness is in a sense the same as true wisdom. The one who is truly wise, and who uses the forces and powers with which he is endowed, to him the great universe always opens her treasure house.

Are you out of a situation? Let the fear that you will not get another take hold of and dominate you, and the chances are that it may be a long time before you will get another, or the one that you do get may be a very poor one indeed. Whatever the circumstances, you must realize that you have within you forces and powers that you can set into operation that will triumph over any and all apparent or temporary losses. Set these forces into operation and you will then be placing a magnet that will draw to you a situation that may be far better than the one you have lost, and the time may soon come when you will be even thankful that you lost the old one.

Recognize, working in and through you, the same Infinite Power that creates and governs all things in the universe, the same Infinite Power that governs the endless systems of worlds in space. Send out your thought, — thought is a force, and it has occult power of unknown proportions when rightly used and wisely directed, —send out your thought that the right situation or the right work will come to you at the right time, in the right way, and that you will recognize it when it comes. Hold to this thought, never allow it to weaken, hold to it, and continually water it with firm expectation. You in this way put your advertisement into a psychical, a spiritual newspaper, a paper that has not a limited circulation, but one that will make its way not only to the utmost bounds of the earth, but of the very universe itself. It is an advertisement, moreover, which if rightly placed on your part, will be far more effective than any advertisement you could possibly put into any printed sheet, no matter what claims are made in regard to its being "the great advertising medium."

In the degree that you come into this realization and live in harmony with the higher laws and forces, in that degree will you be able to do this effectively. If you wish to look through the "want" columns of the newspapers, then do it, but not in the ordinary way. Put the higher forces into operation and thus place it on a higher basis.

If you get the situation and it does not prove to be exactly what you want, if you feel that you are capable of filling a better one, then the moment you enter upon it take the attitude of mind that this situation is the stepping-stone that will lead you to one that will be still better. Hold this thought steadily, affirm it, believe it, expect it, and all the time be faithful, absolutely faithful to the situation in which you are at present placed. If you are not faithful to it then the chances are that it will not be the stepping-stone to something better, but to something poorer. If you are faithful to it, the time may soon come when you will be glad and thankful, when you will rejoice, that you lost your old position.

From The Law and the Word
by Thomas Troward
ISBN: 1-60459-065-3

The correction which our mode of thinking needs therefore is to start with Being, not with Having, and we may then trust the Having to come along in its right order; and if we can get into this new manner of thinking, what a world of worry it will save us! If we realize that the Law flows from the Word, and not vice versa, then the Law of attraction must work in this manner, and will bring to us all those conditions through which we shall be able to express the more expanded Being towards which we are directing our Word; and as a consequence, we shall have no need to trouble about forcing particular conditions into existence—they will grow spontaneously out of the seed we have planted. All we have to do now, or at any time, is to take the conditions that are ready to hand and use them on the lines of the sort of "being" towards which we are directing our Thought—use them just as far as they go at the time, without trying to press them further—and we shall find by experience that out of the present conditions thus used to-day, more favourable conditions will grow in a perfectly natural manner to-morrow, and so on, day by day, until, when later on we look back, we shall be surprised to find ourselves expressing all, and more than all, the sort of "being" we had thought of. Then, from this new standpoint of our being, we shall continue to go on in the same way, and so on *ad infinitum*, so that our life will become one endless progress, ever widening as we go on. And this will be found a very quiet and peaceful way, free from worry and anxiety, and wonderfully effective. It may lead you to some position of authority or celebrity; but as such things belong to the category of "Having" and not of "Being" they were not what you aimed at, and are only by-products of what you have become in yourself. They are conditions, and like all other conditions should be made use of for the development of still more expanded "being"; that is to say, you will go on working on the more extended scale which such a position makes possible to you. But the one thing you would not try to do with it would be to "boss the show." The moment you do this you are no longer using the Word of the larger Personality, and have descended to your old level of the smaller personality, just John Smith or Mary Jones, ignorant of yourselves as being anything greater. It is true your Word still directs the operation of the Law towards yourself—it always does this—but your word has become inverted, and so calls into operation the Law of Contraction instead of the Law of Expansion. A higher position means a wider field for usefulness—that is all; and to the extent to which you fit yourself for it, it will come to you. So, if you content yourself with always speaking in your Thought the Creative Word of "Being" from day to day, you will find it the Way of Peace and the Secret of a Happy Life—by no means monotonous, for all sorts of unexpected interests will be continually opening out to you, giving you scope for all the activities of which your present degree of "being" renders you capable. You will always find plenty to do, and find pleasure in doing it, so you need never be afraid of feeling dull.

From The Master Key System
by Charles F. Haanel
ISBN: 1-934451-31-2

But we shall find that there is a vast difference between simply thinking, and directing our thought consciously, systematically and constructively; when we do this we place our mind in harmony with the Universal Mind, we come in tune with the Infinite, we set in operation the mightiest force in existence, the creative power of the Universal Mind. This, as everything else, is governed by natural law, and this law is the "Law of Attraction," which is that Mind is creative, and will automatically correlate with its object and bring it into manifestation.

This, then, is the way we are consistently creating and recreating ourselves; we are today the result of our past thinking, and we shall be what we are thinking today, the Law of Attraction is bringing to us, not the things we should like, or the things we wish for, or the things some one else has, but it brings us "our own," the things which we have created by our thought processes, whether consciously or unconsciously. Unfortunately, many of us are creating these things unconsciously.

Every form of life attracts to itself the necessary material for growth. The oak, the rose, the lily, all require certain material for their most perfect expression and they secure it by silent demand, the Law of Attraction, the most certain way for you to secure what you require for your most complete development.

Make the Mental Image; make it clear, distinct, perfect; hold it firmly; the ways and means will develop; supply will follow the demand; you will be led to do the right thing at the right time and in the right way. Earnest Desire will bring about Confident Expectation, and this in turn must be reinforced by Firm Demand. These three cannot fail to bring about Attainment, because the Earnest Desire is the feeling, the Confident Expectation is the thought, and the Firm Demand is the will, and, as we have seen, feeling gives vitality to thought and the will holds it steadily until the law of Growth brings it into manifestation.

Is it not wonderful that man has such tremendous power within himself, such transcendental faculties concerning which he had no conception? Is it not strange that we have always been taught to look for strength and power "without?" We have been taught to look everywhere but "within" and whenever this power manifested in our lives we were told that it was something supernatural.

There are many who have come to an understanding of this wonderful power, and who make serious and conscientious efforts to realize health, power and other conditions, and seem to fail. They do not seem able to bring the Law into operation. The difficulty in nearly every case is that they are dealing with externals. They want money, power, health and abundance, but they fail to realize that these are effects and can come only when the cause is found.

Those who will give no attention to the world without will seek only to ascertain the truth, will look only for wisdom, will find that this wisdom will unfold and disclose the source of all power, that it will manifest in thought and purpose which will create the external conditions desired. This truth will find expression in noble purpose and courageous action.

Create ideals only, give no thought to external conditions, make the world within beautiful and opulent and the world without will express and manifest the condition which you have within. You will come into a realization of your power to create ideals and these ideals will be projected into the world of effect.

For instance, a man is in debt. He will be continually thinking about the debt, concentrating on it, and as thoughts are causes the result is that he not only fastens the debt closer to him, but actually creates more debt. He is putting the great law of Attraction into operation with the usual and inevitable result — Loss leads to greater "Loss."

What, then, is the correct principle? Concentrate on the things you want, not on the things you do not want. Think of abundance; idealize the methods and plans for putting the Law of Abundance into operation. Visualize the condition which the Law of Abundance creates; this will result in manifestation.

If the law operates perfectly to bring about poverty, lack and every form of limitation for those who are continually entertaining thoughts of lack and fear, it will operate with the same certainty to bring about conditions of abundance and opulence for those who entertain thoughts of courage and power.

This is a difficult problem for many; we are too anxious; we manifest anxiety, fear, distress; we want to do something; we want to help; we are like a child who has just planted a seed and every fifteen minutes goes and stirs up the earth to see if it is growing. Of course, under such circumstances, the seed will never germinate, and yet this is exactly what many of us do in the mental world.

We must plant the seed and leave it undisturbed. This does not mean that we are to sit down and do nothing, by no means; we will do more and better work then we have ever done before, new channels will constantly be provided, new doors will open; all that is necessary is to have an open mind, be ready to act when the time comes.

Thought force is the most powerful means of obtaining knowledge, and if concentrated on any subject will solve the problem. Nothing is beyond the power of human comprehension, but in order to harness thought force and make it do your bidding, work is required.

Remember that thought is the fire that creates the steam that turns the wheel of fortune, upon which your experiences depend.

Ask yourself a few questions and then reverently await the response; do you not now and then feel the self with you? Do you assert this self or do you follow the majority? Remember that majorities are always led, they never lead. It was the majority that fought, tooth and nail, against the steam engine, the power loom and every other advance or improvement ever suggested.

For your exercise this week, visualize your friend, see him exactly as you last saw him, see the room, the furniture, recall the conversation, now see his face, see it distinctly, now talk to him about some subject of mutual interest; see his expression change, watch him smile. Can you do this? All right, you can; then arouse his interest, tell him a story of adventure, see his eyes light up with the spirit of fun or excitement. Can you do all of this? If so, your imagination is good, you are making excellent progress.

Printed in the United States
98361LV00003B/216/A